Praise for ... *And a Poem*

Refreshingly Sweet A refreshingly sweet and simple rendition of God's Word. This would be an excellent instrument for a Bible study group or a young adult religion class. The poetry captures the spirit of the stories with the brightness and love that illuminates the spirit and love of God throughout. Excellent reading!!!

DARCIE JOHNSON

A Lyrical Trip through the Word I loved reliving God's history with His creation (past present and future) through Kathy's wonderful word pictures. Can't wait for the next volume!

SUSAN

I enjoyed reading this book by a very talented and creative writer. A wonderful book and I look forward to reading more from her in the future. I recommend this book to those who love poetry.

AMY M. GRIGGS

...And a Poem, Too

*More Creative Inspirations
from the Good Book*

Kathy Mansfield

DEKALB, ILLINOIS

... And a Poem, Too.
Visit www.andapoem.com

Copyright © 2015 by April Kathleen Mansfield. All rights reserved.

Scripture quotations are taken from the *Holy Bible, New Living Translation*, copyright © 1996, 2004, 2007, 2013. Used by permission of Tyndale House Publishers, Inc., Carol Stream, Illinois 60188. All rights reserved.

Cover image depicts Accordance Mobile from OakTree Software, www.accordancebible.com.

Cover image copyright © 2015 by Richard Mansfield. All rights reserved.

bookgenesis™ is a trademark of Black Earth Group, Inc., www.blackearthgroup.com.

For my mom, Dottie Bennett

In memory of my brother, Clark Putman and my grandmother, Myrtle Stafford

Contents

Foreword	11

Old Testament

Melchizedek	14
Sodom and Gomorrah	15
The Ten Commandments	17
Rahab	18
Achan	20
As For Me and My House	22
Jael's Peg	23
Esther	25
Psalm 23	28
Psalm 139	30
Proverbs	31
Last Call?	32
Ezekiel, the Prophet	33
Ezekiel's Mission	34
Valley of Dry Bones	36

The Writing on the Wall	39
Hezekiah	42

New Testament

Eating With Scum	44
The Great Commission	45
Jesus Heals a Paralyzed Man	46
Parable of the Fool	48
Incognito Jesus	50
The Stoning	53
Doubting Thomas	55
Ananias and Sapphira	57
Who Saw Jesus?	58
Don't Worry	59
Love of Money	60
Pay Attention	61
Hebrews 11	62

Topics

Addiction	68
Bob, the Last Disciple	69
Devil's Door	71
God's Will	72
Hitting Close to Home	73
Hope	74
Life's Scars	75

Mammaw's Bible	76
More Than a Prayer	77
New Year's Resolution	78
Orthodoxy Lives	80
Priorities?	81
Realms	83
Remember the Sabbath	84
Security	85
Simmering in My Faith	86
Stumbling Block?	87
Ten-Dollar Words	88
When Bad Things Happen	89

Foreword

"Want to hear my new poem?"

This is the question I get every Sunday on the way home from church. Sometimes Kathy's written two: one based on the lesson I taught in our Sunday School class and one from our pastor's sermon. I suppose I'll know that he and I have started to repeat ourselves when Kathy can't write new poems based on our messages.

As I described in Kathy's first poetry book, *...And a Poem*, her unique way of taking notes when listening to a sermon or taking part in a Bible study is to put what she has learned to rhyme. And although I'm admittedly biased, she still amazes me. I wish I had such creativity—especially at the speed with which Kathy can compose a new poem.

Kathy's been known to accept challenges. "Well, you don't have a poem on Hebrews 11," I told her one Saturday afternoon. She had written it within an hour, and you'll find it within the pages of this book. Family members have begun contacting her when there's an upcoming special occasion, asking for a suitable poem. She's become our personal poet laureate.

Mostly new to this volume, you'll find a section of topical poems related to the Bible. Kathy actually writes on all kinds of topics, so be on the lookout in coming months for yet a third volume of her poetry, but with a more diverse subject matter. In the meantime, enjoy this new volume of Kathy's Bible study notes set to meter and rhyme.

Rick Mansfield
September 9, 2015
Simpsonville, Kentucky

Old Testament

... AND A POEM, TOO

Melchizedek

Genesis 14
Hebrews 5; 6; 7

Melchizedek, King of Salem,
And priest of God Most High,
Greeted Abram after war
And brought him bread and wine.

Melchizedek gave a blessing
To Abram from the Lord;
Abram gave a tenth of goods
His victories had restored.

Melchizedek is remembered
As resembling God's own Son;
He wasn't Who would come,
But an example of the One.

Jesus is the final priest,
Atonement for our sins,
And Melchizedek was there
As the story all begins.

Sodom and Gomorrah

Genesis 18:16–19:29

Sodom and Gomorrah
Were known for wicked ways,
So God prepared a punishment
That would end their very days.

But Abraham asked the Lord,
"Will the righteous perish, too?
What if there are fifty
Who proclaim and worship you?"

The Lord replied to Abraham,
"Yes, if fifty can be found,
I will spare the city
And save the entire town."

Then Abraham cleared his throat
And asked of forty-five:
"Lord, would you still spare them
And keep them all alive?"

... AND A POEM, TOO

And so the Lord acquiesced
And said He'd withhold wrath
If forty-five, then forty,
Down to ten were on His path.

From both of the cities
Only Lot and his small clan
Escaped the rain of fire
Brought down by God's own hand.

KATHY MANSFIELD

The Ten Commandments
Exodus 20:1-17

Follow only God,
Is rule number one;
The second one says,
Idols should be none.

When you use God's name
Show honor, peace, and love;
Remember every Sabbath
For praising God above.

Give honor to your parents;
Value life and wedding vows
Are rules five through seven
From God's list of "thous."

Don't take what isn't yours;
Do testify with truth;
Be content with what you have —
These are God's ten rules.

... AND A POEM, TOO

Rahab
Joshua 2:1-24
Matthew 1:5

Joshua sent two spies
To the city of Jericho
To find out more about
A potential battle foe.

But someone told the King,
"There are spies here in the land;
They're in the house of Rahab,
We need to know their plan."

The King sent word to Rahab,
"Bring out the Israelites!"
She responded, "They aren't here —
Perhaps they've taken flight."

In truth, the men were hidden
Under flax on Rahab's roof.
She knew the God they worshipped
Was the One who spoke the Truth.

"I know your God is mighty,
I've heard all the things he does.
I've given you protection,
Now give the same to us."

The Israelites agreed
When they returned to Jericho
They'd look for Rahab's window —
A scarlet rope hung below.

Due to Rahab's faithfulness
Two spies were saved that day,
And through the line of Rahab
Came the One who is the Way.

... AND A POEM, TOO

Achan
Joshua 7

Dumb old Achan –
He disobeyed the Lord
By confiscating items
He never could afford.

A beautiful robe,
Silver coins, a pound of gold –
If only he had followed
What Israel had been told.

Instead he broke a covenant
By hiding in his sin,
And because of this one man,
Israel's army could not win.

Joshua called upon each tribe
And narrowed by each clan,
Then he narrowed further
By family; then one man.

"Achan, you and yours
Will receive a terrible fate.
For we can't defeat Ai
In a disobedient state."

So, Israel learned a lesson
From Achan's selfish choice,
And chose to obey God
And listen to His voice.

. . . AND A POEM, TOO

As For Me and My House
Joshua 24:14-15

Whom will you serve?
Whose life is your model?
The choice must be made —
Do not pause; do not dawdle.

Do you choose Jesus?
Or do you choose man?
As for me and my house,
We follow God's plan.

Jael's Peg
Judges 4

Sisera was an enemy
In a Hebrew nation war
A fact he would have changed
Had he known what lay in store.

The battles he had won
Made him proud and prone to boast;
He thought Israel would fall
Just as easily as most.

But God had other plans
And used a woman in a tent
To bring a warlord down
And cause a nation to repent.

As Deborah had predicted,
A victory would be won
But not by any man —
By a woman it was done.

... AND A POEM, TOO

Jael called to Sisera:
"Come hide inside my tent.
I'll give you milk to drink,
And they won't know where you went."

Jael grabbed a peg
While Sisera took a nap;
She nailed it through his head
As he lay upon her lap.

As Deborah had predicted
Victory was at hand,
With credit to a woman,
Just as God had planned.

Esther

King Xerxes loved Queen Vashti,
But she defied the King's command;
Her banishment made the way
For saving Jews across the land.

King Xerxes sought another
To wear the Persian crown,
Throughout the land were chosen
Young girls of all renown.

Esther was a Hebrew
Who lived with Mordecai,
Chosen by the royal court,
She caught King Xerxes' eye.

But Haman was an Agagite
And had a grudge with all the Jews,
He made a plan for Xerxes
That would cause the Jews to lose.

. . . AND A POEM, TOO

Though Esther was the Persian Queen,
Her lineage wasn't known,
Even Xerxes who so loved his queen
Was oblivious on his throne.

When Mordecai refused to bow,
Haman set his plan in place.
Xerxes signed the order
To end the Jewish race.

Mordecai warned Esther
Of the plan that would unfold,
Through Hathach he told Esther,
"You must be brave; you must be bold."

"Perhaps you were made queen
For such a time as this.
If you ignore the role you play,
You'll surely be remiss."

So Esther turned to God
In fasting and in prayer
And asked of Mordecai
That the Jews, as well, prepare.

Then Esther went to Xerxes,
And through clever words and deeds,
She turned the course in play
To preserve the Chosen's seed.

Now Haman is no more,
But God's people grow in love,
Thanks to Mordecai and Esther
And providence from above.

Psalm 23
Psalm 23

God is like a shepherd
Providing all I need —
Abundant life and peace
By going where He leads.

God renews my strength
And points me on my way;
By following His lead,
I honor Him each day.

Even when I walk
Through Life's darkest days,
I am not afraid —
I know that He stays.

His shepherd's staff and rod
Protect and comfort me,
I enjoy many blessings
Despite my enemies.

He anoints me for a purpose,
My life is full and blessed,
Goodness, love, and mercy —
Of these I can attest.

Because He is my shepherd
I will live beneath His care,
Forever in His presence,
Adopted as His heir.

Psalm 139
Psalm 139

Lord, you know my head,
You know my inner soul,
You know all of my failures,
All my hopes, all my goals.

I can't escape your Spirit,
Your presence is always near;
North or south and east or west —
You are always here.

You made me in my mother's womb,
Writing all my days,
Search me, know me, test me,
And lead me in your ways.

Proverbs

Proverbs 1:1-7

These are the proverbs of Solomon,
King of Israel, David's Son,
For teaching people wisdom —
The very old, the very young.

Fear of the Lord's the foundation —
The place where knowledge resides;
Using that knowledge for good
Is what the wisest of men decides.

The foolish man will just ignore
The discipline, insight, and words —
He'll listen, he'll read, he'll acknowledge,
But his life shows he never heard.

The wise man, however, succeeds
By listening then doing what's right.
He does what he's learned from the Lord
And moves out of darkness to light.

... AND A POEM, TOO

Last Call?
Proverbs 23:29-35

Who has anguish? Who has sorrow?
Who complains and fights?
Whose eyes are always bloodshot?
Who has bruises every night?

It is the one who lingers
In the taverns and the bars,
Trying out new drinks
And toasting to the stars.

In the end that drinking
Turns and bites him like a snake;
He sees what isn't there,
His hands appear to shake.

He staggers like a sailor
Clinging to a swaying mast
And says, "What happened to me?"
Yet, this drink won't be his last.

KATHY MANSFIELD

Ezekiel, the Prophet

Ezekiel taught by parables,
By allegory, by dirge,
And even listed Judah's sins
To end the evil scourge.

His vision of the temple
Restored for all the land
And a life-giving stream
Finally helped some understand.

The watchman spent his days
As a vessel of the Lord
So that God's chosen ones
Might some day be restored.

... AND A POEM, TOO

Ezekiel's Mission

Ezekiel saw an angel
And fell down on his face.
"Surely, this is God
Who greets me in this place!"

Ezekiel saw a wheel
Turning to and fro
And lights like burning flames
And, so he bowed down low.

"Stand up, mortal man.
I want to speak to you!"
Came the voice of God
Whose Spirit came down, too.

"The rebel nation Israel
Is stubborn through and through.
They must know that I am God,
And so I'm sending you."

"Give them all my message,
But be ready for their scorn.
Their hearts are hard and cold,
And for this they'll surely mourn."

"You will be a watchman;
You'll hear from me, then speak.
The goal will be repentance,
But many will be weak."

"For a remnant, I'll remain,
Then for everyone I'll send
The future Son of Man
Who'll bring glory in the end."

. . . AND A POEM, TOO

Valley of Dry Bones
Ezekiel 37:1-14

Ezekiel was transported
By the Spirit of the Lord
To a valley filled with bones
That he and God explored.

The bones were dry and scattered
With no life that could be found.
God asked his priest-turned-prophet,
"Can these bones rise from the ground?"

"You alone can answer, Lord,"
Was Ezekiel's quick reply.
Then God said, "Speak this message,
'Dry Bones, get up and rise!'"

And then a noisy rattle
Echoed up from valley depths
As bone attached to bone,
And muscles formed with flesh.

Then God asked of his prophet,
"Speak out to Earth's four winds:
Breathe life into these bones
So they may live again."

So Ezekiel spoke the message,
And breath filled up those bones,
And an army of new men
Arose like Israel's clones.

They said to one another,
"We've become so dry and old.
All hope is gone; our nation's dead,
Our very life's grown cold."

Then God told his great prophet,
"Tell the people what I'll do.
I'll open graves of exile
And make everything brand new."

... AND A POEM, TOO

"And when Israel is restored,
My people will proclaim:
'This was from the Lord!
Our nation's been reclaimed!'"

KATHY MANSFIELD

The Writing on the Wall
Daniel 5

King Belshazzar loved feasts
And drinking wine from golden cups,
He took the temple vessels
For each noble as he sups.

As the king and all his nobles
(And their concubines and wives)
Drank from holy goblets
They praised their gods of lies.

Suddenly a hand appeared
And wrote words upon the wall;
King Belshazzar fell to his knees
And to his wise men made a call:

"Who can read this writing
And tell me what it means?
To him I'll give high honor —
He'll be third to me, the king!"

...AND A POEM, TOO

When none of them could read it,
The Queen approached the king,
"There is a man named Daniel
Who's been known to do such things."

So, Daniel (Judah's exile)
Spoke to the king and said,
"Keep your gifts. I'll tell you
What others haven't read.

"Since you've defied the Lord
And praised idols in His stead,
Yahweh's sent a message,
And this is what it said:

"'Your days are numbered here,
You've been weighed and found unfit.
Your kingdom's been divided —
Medes and Persians conquer it.'"

Daniel knew the meaning
And was made a ruler, too.
That night the king was killed
And a new one rose to rule.

Hezekiah

The Book of Hezekiah
Little known and hard to find
Go ahead, take a look —
Satisfy your mind!

Although the monarch heard
God's word and did his work
His name atop a book
Was simply not a perk!

New Testament

... AND A POEM, TOO

Eating With Scum
Matthew 9:9-13

"Why does your teacher eat with such scum?"
Asked the Pharisees one day.
For with the disciples sat Jesus
Amid sinners led astray.

When Jesus heard this question,
He gave this simple reply,
"Healthy folks don't need my help —
It's the sick who need my guide."

"Now, go and learn this scripture:
'Show mercy to those in need;
Forget the burning sacrifice' —
I answer the sinner's plea."

The Great Commission
Matthew 28:16-20

The disciples left for Galilee
Where Jesus told them to go,
They saw him and they worshipped him
(Some doubted even so).

Jesus told his followers,
"I have authority over all.
Now go and make disciples —
Every nation, large and small."

"Baptize them and teach them
To obey all my commands;
And be sure of this, I tell you,
I am with you to the end."

... AND A POEM, TOO

Jesus Heals a Paralyzed Man
Mark 2:1-12

While Jesus taught
In a Capernaum home,
The crowd grew large —
No room to roam.

Four men arrived
With a paralyzed man
To lay before Jesus —
That was the plan.

But, the crowd was so thick
The men were perplexed;
What could they do?
Well, here's what came next:

The four men decided
To climb on the roof
And dig a big hole
(They knew they'd see proof!)

Proof of their faith
In Jesus as Lord,
Proof that their friend
Would be healed and restored.

"Your sins are forgiven,"
Jesus said to the man,
But the religious folks said,
"Oh, no. Only God can!"

So, Jesus replied
"Why let your hearts ask:
Forgiveness or healing?
What's the easier task?"

"Stand up!" said Jesus,
"And pick up your mat!"
Then out the man walked
While onlookers gasped.

Parable of the Fool
Luke 12:15-21

A rich man had a fertile farm;
It produced an abundance of crops.
He said to himself, "What should I do?
My harvest never stops!"

He said to himself, "Here's what I'll do —
I'll tear down all of my barns.
I'll build the largest in the land
And be the envy of other farms!"

"Then I'll sit back and say to myself,
'Look at all that you have stored!
Enough to last for many a year —
More than your neighbors could afford!'"

"'Now, take it easy; eat and drink;
Be merry and worry no more!'"
But God said to him, "You foolish man.
When you die, who gets what you've stored?"

KATHY MANSFIELD

A foolish man stores up his wealth
And thinks of only himself.
His relationship with God is poor,
And his riches fade with his health.

...AND A POEM, TOO

Incognito Jesus
Luke 24:15-34

Two followers of Jesus
Walked the Emmaus Road
Discussing all that happened
To the Messiah once foretold.

Suddenly a man appeared
And walked along beside
(The man was really Jesus
Whom they didn't recognize).

The stranger (really Jesus)
Asked of what they spoke,
With sadness they replied,
"How can you not know?"

"Jesus, the man from Nazareth,
Was a prophet who taught us well.
He performed many miracles
And bid us all to tell."

"But our religious leaders
Condemned this man to die.
We wonder now, 'Was he the one?
Or was this just a lie?'"

"Some women of our group
Claimed Jesus had arose,
And sure enough his body was gone,
Just as they had told."

The stranger (really Jesus)
Was bewildered at their talk,
"You foolish people, don't you know?"
Then he taught them as they walked.

Through the writings of Moses
And other prophets, too,
The stranger (really Jesus)
Explained all that was true.

...AND A POEM, TOO

And when they neared Emmaus
He acted as if to leave,
But the men insisted that he stay
And they all sat down to eat.

The stranger (really Jesus)
Blessed the bread and gave it out,
And suddenly the men both knew
Of what he talked about.

The stranger (really Jesus)
Disappeared from their view,
And the men proclaimed to others,
"Believe in the Good News."

The Stoning
John 8:1-11

"This woman was caught;
Let's stone her!" they said.
"Our religious laws
Have all been read."

Jesus responded
To the Pharisee mob,
"All right, throw stones,
But, one caveat:"

"Only throw stones
If you can say
'I've no sin
For which to pay.'"

So, one by one
Each accuser left;
No one stood by
To sentence her death.

...AND A POEM, TOO

"Where did they go?
Does no one condemn?"
Said Jesus to her
Of the Pharisee men.

"No, Lord," she said.
And Jesus replied,
"I don't condemn, either.
To your sin you must die."

KATHY MANSFIELD

Doubting Thomas
John 20:24-29

Thomas was a doubter
(We've learned that from our youth),
Until he saw the nail-scarred hands,
He wavered on the truth.

But calling Thomas "doubting"
May be a bit unjust,
For had I been in his place,
I might have not shown trust.

Thomas simply needed
To see with his own eyes
The risen Lord and Savior
Who came to save our lives.

Isn't that just like us?
Wanting evidence that proves?
Asking for a sign, a word,
Before we make our moves?

...AND A POEM, TOO

If Thomas was a doubter,
Then so are most of us,
But how blessed are all of those
For whom faith is just enough.

Ananias and Sapphira
Acts 5:1-11

Ananias and Sapphira:
A cautionary tale —
A fatal consequence
When truth did not prevail.

Ananias and Sapphira
Kept their offering from the Lord
Instead of sharing all they had,
They chose to lie and hoard.

Ananias and Sapphira
Paid a costly price indeed
For disobeying God
And displaying all their greed.

Ananias and Sapphira
Given sentences to die;
Instead of just obeying,
They resorted to a lie.

... AND A POEM, TOO

Who Saw Jesus?
1 Corinthians 15:4-9

Jesus Christ was buried,
Then He rose up from the grave,
Seen by Peter and the Twelve
Whose lives to Christ they gave.

Then seen by many others —
Five hundred, maybe more,
Then seen by James and later on
By the Apostles He adored.

Then seen at last by Paul
Along the Damascus Road —
An Apostle humbled to his knees
On whom God's grace bestowed.

Now seen by all who come
To His throne of grace and love,
Who trust their hearts and lives
To the One who reigns above.

Don't Worry
Philippians 4:6-9

Don't worry — pray;
Thank God for all He's done.
God will send His peace —
Your worries will be none.

Fix your thoughts on what is true
And honorable and right,
And pure, lovely, admirable,
Then peace will calm your plight.

Love of Money
1 Timothy 6:6-10

True godliness with contentment
Is in itself the greatest wealth,
I brought nothing into this world
And leave it with nothing but myself.

If I've food upon my table
And clothing to keep me warm,
Then I will be content in life
And can weather all Life's storms.

People who long to be rich
Are trapped by harmful desires;
The love of money (Evil's root)
Allows sorrows to transpire.

Pay Attention
Hebrews 2:1-4

Listen very carefully
So you do not drift away;
The message from our God
Is firm in every way.

We cannot just ignore
The One Whom God has sent,
Who delivered life salvation
To all who will repent.

Hebrews 11

Faith is the confidence
That what we hope for will come true
Giving us assurances
Of things we cannot view.

Because of their faith
The people in days of old
Earned a reputation
For trusting what's foretold.

By faith we understand
That by a word from God alone
The universe was formed
Out of things that were unknown.

Abel had that faith
And his offering pleased the Lord
And his example is just one
Showing faith's just reward.

Enoch had that faith;
As a result he didn't die;
Because he pleased the Lord,
He was taken up on high.

Noah had that faith
And chose to build an ark;
He believed what God had warned
And told his family to embark.

Abraham had faith
When God called him from his home
He obeyed and went at once;
For God he chose to roam.

Both Isaac and then Jacob
Had faith like Abraham
Looking forward to a city
Ruled by God's only lamb.

... AND A POEM, TOO

Sarah had that faith
And conceived a little boy
And from his very seed
The world encountered joy.

All these people died
Believing in God's word
They didn't see the end,
But had faith in what they heard.

By faith an only son
Was brought for sacrifice
Abraham believed
God could bring him back to life.

By faith that son named Isaac
Gave blessings for his sons
And Jacob passed that on
To Joseph's little ones.

KATHY MANSFIELD

By faith God's servant Joseph
Believed the Israelites
Would leave the land of Egypt,
And indeed they all took flight.

By faith the baby Moses
Was hidden for three months
And grew to be a prince
Who saved his people more than once.

By faith the Red Sea parted
And God's people saw dry ground
When Egyptians tried to follow
Every one of them was drowned.

By faith the Israel nation
Marched for seven days,
And the walls of Jericho
Fell beneath their praise.

By faith the harlot Rahab
Gave shelter to God's spies
And she alone was saved
When her city heard Death's cries.

By faith so many others
Whose stories could be told
Earned a reputation
For being brave and bold.

Yet none of them received
The promise that they knew
A promise we embrace
Thanks to a faithful few.

Topics

Addiction

I have an addiction
I can't shake and never will,
But it's not one of the bottle
Or of money or of pills.

It's an addiction to the Bible —
To the reading of God's Word;
Can't spend a day without it;
I know it sounds absurd!

I fell off of the wagon once
But verses swarmed my brain;
Although I read no printed words,
The words of God remained.

So, good-bye twelve-step programs;
No counseling for me!
I'll stick with my addiction
'Cause this addiction sets me free!

Bob, the Last Disciple

Bob, the last disciple,
Never made the final cut.
He knew the "where" and "how"
But not the "why" and "what."

Bob knew where Jesus was
And knew how to call his name
But what to do and why
Were out of Bob's domain.

Had someone just said, "Bob,
Give all you have to Christ,"
Then Bob would know the what
To receive eternal life.

Had someone just said, "Bob,
Your life will change for good,"
Then Bob would know the why
To do the thing he should.

... AND A POEM, TOO

So, now you will see Bob
At church each month, each week,
You'll hear him call God's name
As tears flow down his cheek.

But, Bob has never offered
His whole life to Christ the King;
He doesn't know the why
For giving everything.

KATHY MANSFIELD

Devil's Door

The devil's door is wide
And it's open all the time
He beckons all to come
No matter what the crime.

Did I hear some gossip
Or some lies upon your lips?
One stumble can become
The first of many slips.

Once that door is open
The devil holds it fast,
He wants that open door
To be your very last.

But God controls the wind —
Shuts the door in Satan's face,
And wraps us in His arms
So we can feel His grace.

God's Will

God's will for my life
Is plain as any day:
Read the Bible, go to church,
Worship Him and pray.

When I do those things,
I plainly see God's plan
And know the right direction
Guided by His hand.

Making Godly choices
Becomes easier each day;
I ask, "Would God be pleased?"
If so, I'm on my way.

God's will for my life
Is not some mystery;
It's revealed in His word
For all mankind to see.

KATHY MANSFIELD

Hitting Close to Home

When godly people sin,
They need a place to land —
A place of love and grace
To help them rise and stand.

When godly people sin,
They don't need a look of scorn;
They need the open arms
Of those who'll help them mourn.

When godly people sin,
It hits us close to home –
And that's the very reason
We help them not to roam.

Hope

Shake the dust off of your feet
When you leave a life of sin;
Look forward with all hope,
Not back at where you've been.

Life's Scars

If ever someone has been broken and fixed
I think it would be I.
And lo, and behold, I figured out
The answer to my "Why?"

Sometimes God must let us fall
And feel Life's harshest wrath,
Only then can we arise
To walk straighter on His path.

To others I might seem to be
Someone whose life is marred,
But God sees me as clean and new,
Not as someone scarred.

. . . AND A POEM, TOO

Mammaw's Bible

In memory of Queenie Pennington

Mammaw's Bible — cracked and worn —
Holds secrets to her life,
Doting mother, loyal friend,
Pappaw's loving wife.

The turning of each page
Reveals her thoughts and prayers,
Brackets 'round a verse,
Notes jotted here and there.

Tucked between the chapters:
Clippings of years gone by —
Interests, thoughts, and humor,
And poems to make you cry.

But most of all her Bible tells
Her children and her friends,
She read it, and she lived it
Until the very end.

KATHY MANSFIELD

More Than a Prayer

A mentor's like a parent
Who loves and molds and guides,
Who cautions with kind words
And never leaves your side.

A mentor's not a pleaser –
Saying things we want to hear;
A mentor wisely speaks
And always lends an ear.

Good mentors seek from God
Discernment for their life;
They pass along God's words;
They love in times of strife.

God, help me be a mentor
To those who feel despair;
Help me show your mercy
Through more than just a prayer.

New Year's Resolution

My New Year's resolution
Was to read the Bible through,
Both Old and New Testaments –
Maps, concordance, too.

Day one went really well –
The story of creation,
Followed by the ark,
In my best translation.

In those first few weeks
I read of Moses and the law,
The Ten Commandment tablets
And the blessings Israel saw.

But, along about day thirty,
Leviticus came in view,
All those rules and sacrifices
And offering guidance, too.

Instead of easy stories,
I was faced with rules of old,
And my New Year's reading challenge
Started growing pretty cold.

So, here I am, once again,
Stalled before Book Four,
Maybe when the next year comes,
I'll read a little more.

But, here will be my plan
From day one of that new year:
Start with Revelation
And work backward from the rear.

And maybe I might see
By looking at the end
The value of Leviticus
And the message that it sends.

. . . AND A POEM, TOO

Orthodoxy Lives

Orthodoxy's dead
When routine is the norm:
Take the offering, bow your heads,
Complete the visitor form.

Orthodoxy lives
When the Spirit moves in men,
And the hands and mouths and hearts
Of God's people shout "Amen!"

Priorities?

I started getting antsy
On the hard wooden pew,
The pastor kept on preaching
All the things that he knew.

I glanced down at my watch
And I fumbled with my purse;
It was such a long service,
Could things get any worse?

And then the invitation
Was several verses long;
Does the pastor wear a watch?
Are they starting a new song?

I've been here one whole hour,
I've got more that I must do:
Lunch with friends, a movie,
And some shopping in there, too!

...AND A POEM, TOO

An hour's way too long
To do any single thing;
If I sit around for hours
It should be with my TV!

Realms

Satan is the chief
Of the fallen angel realm,
And his minions have the goal
Of being at your helm.

But Jesus is the chief
Of the realm that will survive,
And His people know that hope
Because He is alive.

Remember the Sabbath

When I was growing up,
Sunday was God's holy day.
Don't work, don't shop, don't drink;
Only worship, rest, and pray.

Nowadays that's different —
Sunday's filled with "come and go":
Soccer games, outlet malls,
The latest movie show.

Maybe I am pining
For archaic times and ways,
But I think there was some good
In a day of rest and praise.

'Cause when we stop and pause
And we catch our breath and rest,
We hear God's plan for us
And remember how we're blessed.

Security

Highs and lows
Peaks and valleys
Yet God remains secure;
No matter what we go through,
With Him we can endure.

... AND A POEM, TOO

Simmering in My Faith

At "Microwave Church"
I get just what I need,
Packaged with a smile
And delivered with all speed.

At "Slow Cooker Church"
I consider what I hear,
I examine Holy Scripture,
Asking God to make it clear.

In this pressure cooker life,
I'm glad to have a place
Where I can worship God
At a thoughtful, calming pace.

Stumbling Block?

If what you do in life
Makes others trip and fall,
Then what you do in life
Is not of God at all.

Godly men and women
Encourage, love, and pray;
They choose to walk beside,
Not get in others' way.

... AND A POEM, TOO

Ten-Dollar Words

Sanctification, propitiation —
Big ten-dollar words —
If you grew up in a Bible church,
They're words you must have heard.

Sanctification simply means
Living out your faith,
Growing more like Christ
As you journey through your days.

Propitiation simply means
Atonement for our sins
Resulting from the sacrifice
Of Jesus for all men.

Knowing those big words
Won't change how we should live,
But knowing what they mean
Reminds us why we live.

KATHY MANSFIELD

When Bad Things Happen

When bad things happen to me,
Is it due to my own sin?
Or do bad things sometimes happen
"Just because" and "now and then"?

A God who authors good
Can't also author evil,
But permissive will exists
And can lead to much upheaval.

So when I stub my toe
Or fall and hurt my knee,
That's just a bad occurrence,
Not punishment on me.

Of course, there will be times
When consequences come —
Actions for my sins
And the things that I have done.

...AND A POEM, TOO

Knowing there's a difference
Can help me understand:
Was this the will of God
Or result of sinful man?

www.ingramcontent.com/pod-product-compliance
Lightning Source LLC
Chambersburg PA
CBHW021134300426
44113CB00006B/428